AF479928

The BEAUTY of ALL COLORS

Story by
Reesha Sanghani

Illustrated by
Leela Sanghani

To my daughter Leela and son Arin,
who inspire me to love
everyone for who they are,
and to my husband Neil,
who loves us with a deep and fierce loyalty.

—Reesha Sanghani

Every month is special.
Every month is unique.
Each one is filled with color.
Come and take a peek!

JANUARY first is New Year's Day.
Fireworks light up the night.
The colors all sparkle so brightly.
We shout OOOH and AHHHH with delight!

It's Valentine's Day in FEBRUARY
when we show our love for others.
We share pink and red cards and candy
with our friends, our sisters and brothers.

Love you
Kiss me
All Mine
Hug me
Smile
you Shine
Thank you

MARCH dives in like a hawk
with wind and lots of rain,
but it leaves us with colorful rainbows
when the sun peeks out again!

Earth Day comes in APRIL.
We celebrate earth and all it gives,
the blue sky and green grass
and everything that lives.

MAY brings purple flowers
that bloom in the warm weather.
Take out your bikes, balls and games
and we'll all go play together!

In the bright heat of JUNE,
we cool off in the sun.
The sand burns our toes,
but the beach is such fun!

We fly America's flag on the fourth of JULY.
Its colors are red, white and blue.
All countries have colorful flags,
Mexico, India and Brazil to name a few.

In AUGUST, the nights get cooler.
Our garden's harvest is ready to eat.
Cherry tomatoes, sweet corn and watermelon—
colorful foods make a tasty treat!

good Day
Cayn good

In SEPTEMBER we go back to school.
We wear backpacks and clothes that are new.
Our teachers have planned a great school year
with many fun things we will do.

In OCTOBER, the leaves start to change
making trees look like splashes of dye.
They fall off the trees one at a time,
as if they are learning to fly!

In NOVEMBER, we give thanks for earth's bounty
and celebrate the harvest with food.
Our thanksgiving feast makes us grateful,
and our tummies feel oh, so good.

The last month of the year is DECEMBER.
We set out decorations and lights.
They sparkle against the shimmering snow
making our hearts feel so bright.

Each month shows a rainbow of colors
with many ways to celebrate.
We are all part of one big world and family
in a story that will forever be great.

So do not forget you are special
especially the more different you are,
and that ALL PEOPLE AND COLORS are beautiful,
whether they live near or far!